Fix the Problem

and other Life Lessons from a Pragmatic Dad!

By

Curt Liljedahl, M. Ed, D.A.D

Liljedahl

Fix the Problem!

DEDICATION

I would like to dedicate this to my beautiful daughters, Mackenzy and Zari, who make my life complete. Your lives are far from complete which is why I started this project...to help you in life! I would also like to dedicate this to the students I had the privilege of teaching for 28 years in McAllen, TX who allowed me to show them life is more than just science... it's all
PHYSICS BABY!

Special shout out to my proofreaders, but don't blame them if you find mistakes! That's all me!!

Cindy Twait Liljedahl
Maria Trager

FIX THE PROBLEM
AND OTHER LIFE LESSONS FROM A PRAGMATIC DAD!

prag·mat·ic
prag ' madik/
adjective
dealing with things sensibly and realistically in a way that is based on practical rather than theoretical considerations.

These are some observations and pragmatic advice I have discovered all my years as a teacher and father. I am not saying they are all correct and many of them are my opinions and you may not agree with some of them, but I do believe in them and have passed them on to my daughters and students for many years to help them in life.

1. Move every day!

I know we think we are never going to grow old like our parents, but really that is not a bad thing. If all goes according to plan you are going to age and your body will tell you all about it as the years go by. Stretching is very important as you get older. It feels good in the morning and helps keep the stiffness away throughout the day. This might just be an old man thing, but I have found that if I get down on the floor and stretch out my back I feel much better the rest of the day. It's like Yoga, but I call it wallowing (that's a farm kid thing). Just twist your back, spine, arms joints, and legs joints all around. It feels so good. Doesn't hurt to do some core exercises then either. I found that if you keep the "boobs to butt" muscles strong they support your whole middle section and it helps with your posture and that sore lower back thing. Never hurts to do a quick stretch before bedtime too. It relaxes you and keeps your muscles relaxed during the night. Many of these exercises you can find by doing a quick internet search and figuring out what works for you, but it is very important to do it and stick with it.

2. Be a great parent. This should be your most important job.

I have loved being a parent to my daughters. I'm not saying I was perfect, but I tried. Be there in your kid's lives! Don't be the "drop-off" parent....be involved and shape them! As a teacher, I can't tell you how many times I have seen parents picking up their children after school with their phone glued to their ear. No conversation, no eye contact, no interaction. We all have jobs and get tired, but by being with them you are developing a human life!

3. Don't carry a monthly balance on a credit card.

If you are going to have a credit card (which I don't recommend, but I do understand getting a credit score for apartments and all) _**NEVER EVER**_ carry a monthly balance. Pay it off each month! If you do this then you have used their money for free for 30 days. Interest is way too high and the temptation to overspend is huge. The card companies want to lure you in with "cash back" or "airline miles," but trust me...they ALWAYS make money off of you!

4. Learn about investing money early in life. A little now is a lot later. Compound interest is amazing!

Find an online compound interest calculator to show this, it is a very exponential increase! Even Albert Einstein said, " *Compound interest is the 8th wonder of the world. He who understands it ,earns it . He who doesn't , pays it"*. I started my daughters Roth IRAs at age 17 and 21 and someday, when they are 59 1/2 and can draw on this money and I am 6 feet underground, they will appreciate it. It will be a huge amount of $$$. Young people have the one thing every financial "expert" wishes they had, **YOUTH** which equals **TIME** which equals **MONEY**!.

5. Seems to me that the more "rustic" the restaurant the better the BBQ will be.

If you are from Texas or anywhere else with great BBQ you will get this one. There is no "fancy" BBQ! Some of the best BBQ places I have eaten in have smoke on the wall and outdoor pits. Very cool experiences.

6. Education = money. It does not have to be a college education, but get some sort of trade or skill.

College is nice. I had fun. I got two degrees and had a great career, but it's not the only answer. Plumber, carpenter, mechanic, secretary, auto mechanic, or many other professions that don't require 4 year college are also super careers and can pay well, but you need a marketable skill people are willing to pay for. You need to figure out what works for you with the gifts God gave you and try to make a living with it.

7. Always carry jumper cables and a portable air compressor in your car and know how to use them.

I have these in all our cars and my daughters have been taught to use them. I should probably do a refresher course for them once a year. If it is not you who has a dead battery or flat tire then it will be someone else and maybe you can help them. Drivers quite often forget to turn off their headlights which drains their car battery and if you have jumper cables you can help. But be careful! There are lots of weird people out there who prey on helpful people. Also it seems like 90% of all flats I get are slow leaks, so if you can just pump it up with an small $20 air compressor from Wal-Mart or somewhere you can usually drive to a tire shop and get it fixed and you will get on your way quicker. That way you don't have to change the tire yourself. Before either of my daughters were allowed to drive they had to change a tire on the pick-up they were going to drive and learn to jump start it. I know our insurance has twenty- four hour Roadside Assistance service that will come anywhere at any hour of the day or night to fix a flat or jump your car. There is a time and place to use this service, but these are still skills every driver should have just in case you can't contact that service or Daddy. I used to give extra credit points for my physics students if they made a video demonstrating these skills. All sixteen year olds should know how to perform these skills before they start driving.

8. Have a "bucket list" and work towards it.

This is a list of special things in life that make it fun! Your bucket list doesn't have to be expensive or parts of it might be. You might want to visit a special place like Lambeau Field (home of the Green Bay Packers), or doing something crazy like skydiving that you have always wanted to do. Either keep a mental list or write it down! My list is constantly changing! You can change your list whenever you want...it's your list.

As a kid on a farm in Iowa, my #1 was always to experience zero gravity like the astronauts. Who gets to do that?? Well, as a physics teacher, I got the chance to do zero gravity TWICE and now have thirty minutes of Zero-G on the same planes the astronauts train on. It is the most amazing feeling in the world! In the past year I got the chance to do indoor rock climbing, curling on ice, and skeet shooting. All great fun and now marked off my list. Make sure you get some of these done before you get too old. My mother and I went to Machu Picchu in Peru, South America when she turned eighty years old and because of the mountains and high altitude, that adventure was almost too late for her, but she loved it!

9. Work at your marriage both before and during.

I wish all marriages were like the ones on TV. They make it look so easy. It seems like they don't have jobs that cause stress or if the couple fights it is always cute and funny and everything is all better in thirty minutes! I'm here to tell you that's not the real world! First of all, you need to marry the right person for the right reasons and then keep falling in love every day.   Date nights, weekends away, stay-dates (where you dress up, but stay home to save money), are all important parts of a successful and fun marriage. Also, having common goals and being willing to compromise on things is very important. A great marriage is hard work. I understand divorce. Sometimes people change, make wrong decisions, or just grow apart. That can be a part of life, but don't take the easy way out when things get tough. Keep falling in love and working at your marriage.

10. Read for pleasure.

I didn't get this one for a long time. I am a very slow reader. When I was growing up learning differences like dyslexia or other scientific diagnoses were nonexistent...they just called us dumb or slow readers. But I worked my butt off and now I enjoy reading. It takes me to special places and on amazing adventures. It also makes me very sleepy. I finally got into reading when I had little children and there wasn't too much else to do for fear I might wake them up.

11. Best toy I ever bought my daughters cost $1.29

This was a wiffle ball and bat I got at the grocery store. We played for hours in the driveway with sidewalk chalk

bases.   It really helped teach hand-eye coordination.   Kids
don't always need fancy or high priced toys, and you should
get them off the IPad and away from the TV daily too. We
had many electronic learning toys over the years that were a
huge waste of money, but it was the latest and greatest thing
so we fell for it. For our daughters first Christmas we
wrapped up diapers for her under the tree. She loved them
and used them. She was seven months old. It was all she
needed. By far the best gift we ever gave our daughters were
handmade (and free) Harry Potter wands! They loved them
and ran around the house casting spells on everything! They
were sixteen and twenty years old BTW.

12. Spend a little extra money and buy good tools and shoes.

If you make your living using tools, buy good ones. I am
just a garage tinkerer, so I don't need high-end tools, but if
you make your living with tools you need to have good,
dependable tools. There is a time for cheap multi-tool kits.
They make great high school graduation gifts.

Shoes are important too. If you are on your feet all day,
get good, comfortable shoes. There is a time and place for
high fashion shoes, but save your feet in the long run. You
need them to be healthy a long time.

13. Never lose your personal identity or self- respect.

Being a teacher for so many years I witnessed a lot of kids who would change who they were just to fit in with a certain crowd. I understand wanting to have friends, being popular, or just wanting to be a part of something bigger. It is important to socialize. But if you change who you truly are, you are not you! Kids will dress different, act different, and behave differently just to be a part of something, and that simply is not right. Self-respect is the other part of this equation. I have seen young ladies change into someone that their future adult self would not be proud of just to get and keep the attention of a young man. This kind of behavior changes you forever. If you have to dramatically change who you are in order for a person to like you, then you are with the wrong person and chances are pretty good the relationship will not last. If they really want to be with you, they will like or love you for who you are.

14. Travel as much as you can.

Not everyone likes to travel and I really don't blame them. It is expensive, time-consuming, confusing at times, and it can really take you out of your comfort zone. But there is a big, amazing world out there. Whether you are going to different cities, camping at State or National parks, taking a full tour, local weekend trips, or backpacking to a foreign country, it is amazing to see what is out there beyond our backyard. Get out there!!! Don't let little insecurities stop you from traveling either. I had a friend who would not fly. She had never been on a plane before in her life , but she had it in her head that she was scared of flying. That irrational fear cost her two trips to Europe and one to Alaska.

15. Live within your financial means.

This one is huge. You cannot spend more money than you have. The government does and it's wrong, but we can't. That is called going into debt. You might have to use a car loan or home mortgage someday, but don't go overboard and get a car or house that is too much for your income. Don't lease a car either. It is a horrible waste of your money. If you have to lease a vehicle you are driving a car you can't afford. Listen to or read Dave Ramsey.

16. There is a big difference between being adventurous and being irresponsible or stupid.

I love adventure which kind of goes back to #8 and the Bucket List thing, but if you are seeking adventure and you put you or your family in too much danger, that's just stupid. This can be both physical or financial irresponsibility. If you do an adventure you can't afford at that stage of your life OR you get injured on an adventure and it prevents you from earning money to feed yourself or your family then the adventure is owning you. This is not good!

17. See the donut, not the hole.

This is an old analogy, but it means to have a positive mindset in life, not a negative. If I'm not happy, well then what the heck??? Life is going to suck and I don't want that for you or me. We all know those people who piss and moan about everything and seem to pull others down to their level of unhappiness. This might make us feel better about our lives for a little while, but these people are a cancer to be around too much. This positive attitude can be very hard when life is dumping on you, but a positive attitude will always get you farther in life.

18. Change your car oil and filters when you are suppose too and rotate your tires regularly. This saves gas and money!

This is just a physics thing, but any car mechanic will tell you that the best way to make your car last a long time is to change the oil, oil filters, and air filters regularly. Sometimes you may think you can't afford it or you can save a little money by putting it off another month or 1000 miles, but many studies show that a little maintenance cost helps prevent a lot of repair costs. Normal oil is around 3000 miles whereas synthetic oil is 5000 miles. Read your Owner's Manual.

Also, the best way to save gas is to have your tires properly inflated. Usually 32-35 PSI or whatever it says on the inside of the door. This makes the tires last longer too and tires are very expensive. Again, read your Owner's Manual. All the information is there. Another thing is to rotate your tires every 5000-8000 miles so they will last longer. Driving on worn or bad tires is a safety hazard for both you and others on the road around you.

19. Call or visit your parents, grand-parents or other older people in your life.

These people are amazing!!! The stories they tell, the lives they have lived, and the experiences they have had are beautiful. Yes, you may hear the same story over and over, but it is good for them to tell these stories and it is good for us to hear them, especially family history so it gets passed on to the next generation. Their lives were a lot simpler and harder than ours and they have earned our patience and respect. Also, they won't always be here so listen and talk to them while you can. I wish I could talk to my Dad one more time.

20. Look at the moon.

My daughters taught me this one! One Friday night at a football game both my girls (at different times) said, "Daddy, did you see the moon?" Sure enough, it was a full, beautiful, South Texas moon. It made me think that we raised them right! This is the same as the "take time to smell the roses" saying. Don't get so wrapped up in the busy part of life that you forget to see the beauty all around you or life's simple pleasures.

21. Find a job you love doing.

The old saying says "if you love your job, you will never work a day in your life." Easier said than done! I have read that the average working person will have around eleven different jobs in his lifetime. I believe this, because if I consider all the jobs I had in summers (lifeguard, hoeing beans, etc), and then my "real" jobs after college, I suppose I would on the low side, but I did learn you have to love what you're doing or you will hate going to work every day and that makes for a long and miserable career. Having a job you don't like will hurt your personality, too, because you become a bitter person and that will affect how you are seen by others and your health.

22. Shop for sales.

If you know you need to buy something, but you don't need it immediately, wait for a sale. When building our house I knew we needed window coverings on our windows, but we live on a lake so it was not an immediate need. Finally a "Buy one, get one 50% Off" sale happened and I got a $1000 worth of window blinds for $750. Savings= $250. Looking for and waiting for sales is a great way to save money.

23. Be careful about paying Service or Convenience Fees.

My daughter's college recently started charging a "convenience fee" of 2.5% for paying for school with a debit or credit card. That is essentially $2.50 for every $100 spent. That doesn't sound too bad and to most people a 2.5% fee does not seem very big, but when you consider her bill that year for college was $21,000 that 2.5% "convenience fee" is equal to $525 extra we would have to pay. (21000 x .025 = 525) That is not chump change in my world, so we paid with electronic checking which did not have the fee.

ATM machines get you on this too. If the machine is not with your bank you have to agree to a "service charge" of usually $2.00 to $4.00 per transaction. If you are only withdrawing a small amount like $20.00 that makes the charge between 10% and 20% which is huge. So IF you have to pay a service charge it is better to take out more money (if you have it) which makes the service charge percentage less. OR BETTER YET, buy something small at a store like a soda or candy bar and get cash back on your purchase if possible. That way you avoided the fees altogether!

24. Only spout your political opinions in the proper places.

Do you know that person who seems to bring up their political views all the time? For this! Against that! Democrat! Republican! Whatever! *Just shut up!* If we are discussing politics or government then maybe I want to hear your views and I might tell you mine, but if we are at a football game or out to dinner, I don't want to hear it. Don't get me wrong, I know these things are important and I have my opinions too, but there is a time and place for everything.

25. Know the difference between *Wants* and *Needs*.

My wife *Wants* a robotic vacuum for our house. We have a vacuum that works just fine. That is a *Want.* I *Want* to go to Iceland. I really don't *Need* to go to Iceland. *Wants* are a luxury item in our life. Things we can easily do without, but would it be nice or fun to have. *Needs* are food, clothing, shelter, electricity, etc. Hopefully, there will come a point in your life where you can afford to have all your *Wants*, but they should never be a priority. Contrary to popular belief Cell phones are a *Want*, not a need.

26. Take time to pray, meditate, or read.

Life is crazy at times if you haven't already noticed! Things like meetings, work, homework, and family all pile up. All these things stress us out in life. Take some time to relax by praying, meditating, or something that helps you just to cool down and relax. It is said that just taking a forty-five minute walk outside does wonders for you! It works for me anyway!

27. Keep in contact with old friends even if it is through social media.

From what I've seen friends come and go in life. They move on, you move on, jobs change, kids grow up, change schools. Always keep in contact with them. It is fun to get together occasionally and reminisce about the good old days. This has gotten a lot easier now with cell phones, email, and social media.

28. If not now...When??

Setting goals is very important. For example; taking a vacation, going back to school, going camping, investing for your future, starting an IRA, starting a family, etc. Setting the goal is the easy part, actually doing it is the hard part. Life gets in the way quite often and we can not do all the things we want to do when we want to do them, but be sure to responsibly work towards the goals. Don't just pay "lip service" to them because very quickly the time will come when you still want to do these things, but can't. My 101 year old uncle told me once, "Do it now, because everything gets harder at my age."

29. Embrace where you are in life.

Not everyone has a better life than you and if they actually do, well good for them, but that is their life, not yours. Social media doesn't help this at all. Look at what you have and where you are in your life and know that many, many people in the world wish they were in your shoes. While some parts of your life may be bad for a while, other parts are probably pretty good. It's very hard to do, but don't focus on the bad parts. They will just keep sucking your further down. Look at the good parts and work towards having more of them.

30. If you have made really good money on an investment, don't be too greedy. Sell part of it.

I like to invest in stocks. I saw a trendy product one

time and invested early in it. My $3,000 investment quickly turned into $21,000. Yes!!!! I was an investing genius and ahead of the trend, but I got greedy. After a short while, the trend died out, and foreign knock-off products hit the market, and being the great investor I was I rode that investment all the way down to $1,500. Dumb, dumb, dumb! Somewhere on the profitable side I should have sold at least $3,000 worth and saved my original investment. Then all the rest would have been profit.

31. Recycle. It is free or you can even make money.

Where does all our trash go? Dumps, landfills, the ocean? Our earth is filling up! I am not an obsessed Greenpeace warrior, but I am a realist. Plastics and glass do NOT break down so we have been hiding them in these places where they will be forever and we are going to run out of room. *Why not recycle??* At least it is getting used again and again. Some cities make it very easy to recycle. Just put the recyclable trash in the special container, and they do the rest. Even if you have to separate it yourself and take it to a recycle center, it is the right thing to do and sometimes you can make money by selling the aluminum or at least get your deposit back depending on the state you live. Our local town of 400 people collects donated cans for the five cent deposit and raises thousands of dollars for our community. Win - Win!!!

32. Have a garden.   This is a great way to relax and get good food.

I love having a garden. Yes, when you consider the time and money I spend on my garden they could be the most expensive tomatoes I have ever eaten, but to me it is worth it, but this is not always the case.   Our garden is only a small raised four foot by eight foot raised garden box, but we have beans, basil, and tomatoes to eat and share. It is also very relaxing to tend the garden and the food you grow tastes much better than store-bought. Gardens are not for everyone or for everywhere, but they are a good thing. Nobody truly has a "Green Thumb"! If you can read and follow directions, you can garden.

33. Try not to do things in your youth you will regret later in life. Look down the road.

Some of the choices we made when we are young can come back to hurts us when we get older. I am not a big fan of tattoos, but I understand that some people

24

like them for whatever the reason. That's fine... no problems. But when people get tattoos or piercing to reflect the values and beliefs of their youth, the permanence of that decision might (and I said might) affect them into adulthood. For example I used to have long hair when I was young. It was who I was. My friends called me "Wildman". It was not however permanent. As I grew older, long hair did not reflect who I was as a person. I changed and times changed! Also, as an adult I had a career that paid me very good money, and it would not have been possible with the long hair. It was not the "look" my career wanted then. I remember an older gentleman at our church who had a tattoo of a naked lady on his forearm from his days in the Navy when he was young. He was proud of his Navy days, but always wore long sleeved shirts in public because his values had changed and that tattoo was very embarrassing for him in church and also around his granddaughters.

Another quick story about a friend who got arrested on pot possession when he was young. He grew up, got married, became a father, joined the Marines, and did two tours in Afghanistan and Kuwait. A truly great guy, man, husband, and father. After eight years in the Marines, he went to apply for a job with Border Patrol and was rejected because of issues with a MIP (Minor in Possession) when he was in high school.

34. When you are working for a living and have a family get a Will, a Living Will, and a Power of Attorney.

Without a Will some Judge who does not know you or your circumstances gets to make decisions about your estate (money and property) or where your kids will go to live if you die. Too often I hear people say "they will go to so and so because they are their godparents". That means nothing in the eyes of the law and other family members could fight it. Maybe they want your kids (or your money)! If your estate is big and/or complex have a lawyer draw it up. It is good money to have a will done right. If your estate is small and/or simple you can get some wills and the other things online.

35. Life is not fair! I am sorry, but deal with it. The harder it kicks you, the harder you have to fight.

This one sucks, but Life is NOT fair. Example: Why does this happen to me and not them? Why did that person die? Why are they idiots and doing amazing and I am a great guy and struggling? First of all refer back to #29. A lot of time we don't know what is going on behind other peoples' doors. We THINK we do, but we really don't. Their life might not be as great as they make it look on social media.

Secondly..."*Shit happens*". (I apologize for the language). Or maybe I should say "*Life Happens*"! I personally find myself saying "it is what it is" way too often. In MY world I know God has a plan. I don't know what it is, and maybe I might not agree with it, but I do know He has a plan for my life. If you are not a religious person then I guess you just have to go with "life happens". Either way we need to suck it up and roll with the punches and do the best we can in life. It's the only one we have.

36. Be Proactive, not Reactive!

This one is an addendum (an item of additional material) to #35. While we can say "life Happens", I have also heard the expression "make life happen" or "planners have the best luck!" While we are NOT in control of our lives, and we are just kidding ourselves if we think we are, we can help things along by being proactive. You will never get that great job if you are not trained for it or have the proper education. You will also NOT get that job if you don't apply. You won't meet the right people if you don't look for the right people and look in the right places. Your dream girl will not walk in your house, turn off the football game, and ask you out!

Another expression I like is "set yourself up for success". I shudder to think where I would be in life if I hadn't held back my fear when I asked my wife of 32 years out on our first date. If you never swing the bat, you will never hit a homerun and I hit a grand slam!

37. Get out of your comfort zone.

"If you keep doing the wrong thing you will keep getting the wrong results." Push yourself to get out of your "bubble" occasionally and try new things. Don't let life turn into a rut. Go somewhere you want to go. Apply for that dream job. Ask out that person for a date. Don't be afraid to be alone. Push yourself always!

38. If you must use a credit card pay as much as you can monthly and get it paid off fast.

If you use a credit card (I personally recommend only a debit card, but I see the advantages of both), and IF you must carry a balance over (I recommend paying it off EVERY month) pay at least more than the minimum payment to get it paid off as fast as possible. Minimum payments is how they suck you in to using your card more. DON'T DO IT!!! It is a vicious cycle that gets you deeper and deeper into debt with high interest rate. Get online and find a credit card payment calculator that shows you how much <u>principal</u> or "what you borrowed" verses <u>interest</u>, or "what you are paying extra to use that card" and put in your balance and the interest rate. Very scary!

39. Late fees on most credit cards are huge and sometimes very secretly added into your monthly balances. Pay on time.

If you do use credit cards, check your monthly statements. I was doing this once and right there in among all our purchases (hidden very well) was a $39 late fee!!! I thought I had paid on time, but due to auto-pay and computer stuff, my payment was late. It might have been just one day or even one minute, but they charged me. I called the credit card company to try and get them to drop the late fee because sometimes they will if it is your first time. They didn't!!!! They told me they would waive half the fee and drop it to $20, but I was still not happy. I told them if they didn't drop the whole fee I would cancel my card, but they didn't care so in the same phone call I told them I would pay-off my account and for them to close the account. Even that cost $10 for some reason, but after some online research, I had ordered a different card from another company and had it in two days. I don't use credit cards anymore.

40. Never use payday loans, title loans, or gimmicks like that.

This kind of "borrowing" money is poison!! Either you could lose your car (title loan) or you will be paying VERY high interest rates. In some cases interest rates for a 2 week loan can range between 300% to 800%. Just to borrow $100 for 2 weeks could cost you between $15 - $30. They make the TV commercials look all great and easy, but in the case of a Title loan you are literally agreeing to have repo company come in the middle of the night or while you are at a store shopping and repossess your car when you park it if you do not pay them back with huge interest. Bad news!!

41. Always pay extra principal on car and home loans to pay them off earlier.

Find an amortization calculator that you can enter in your loan amounts, interest rates, and how long the loan is for (which can be up to 30+ years), and it will show you an amortization table. These things will really open your eyes to what borrowing money costs. You will notice that in the first half of the loan period the interest amount is a lot higher than the principal amount. The two amounts become about equal around halfway through the loan period, and FINALLY towards the back half of the loan you start paying more for what you borrowed than what it costs you to borrow that money. Again...very scary! Work with the numbers and see for yourself.

Our first home loan we had a 30 year term loan and paid it off in 11 years. Our second home (a rental property) had a 15 year term loan and we paid it off in 6 years. Our 3rd home (and by far the most expensive because it was our dream home on a lake) we paid cash for because the first 2 homes paid for it. SWEET! No house payment and lots of equity (the money we get when we sell the house).

42. If it sounds too good to be true…it usually is.

This is an oldie, but goodie, and it very much holds true today. Now with the Internet and all the offers and deals you can get online it can be very scary. Who do you believe??? Who can you trust?? Please remember this one thing! Nothing is really FREE! Somehow, someway people are going to use you to make a profit. It might only cost you your time or it could cost you your money , but people selling a product or a service will not lose when dealing with you no matter what they say. Don't forget that people will out and out lie to you so they can feed their families. I hate being so cynical, but it's true.

43. Everybody wants your money. If you don't watch it, someone else will.

This one goes hand in hand with #42. If you, and I mean **YOU**, don't watch where your hard earned money goes, someone else will be more than happy to watch it for you. This not only applies to your big stuff like cars and investments, but even paying at a counter for something small. I can't think of how many times I have seen things rung up at the counter wrong or didn't include the sales offer or whatever, and they just tell me how much I owe and expect me to blindly pay. I saw a sale in a big box store one time that was real good. A Bocce Ball set on sale for $5 marked down from $20. Cool I thought. I go to the counter and they ring it up at $20. I said "no, no, no! That's marked down to $5. The teller said "well it rings up at $20". So I got out of line, went back to the display and removed the shelf sticker that had the price on it and brought it back to the same cashier and showed it to her. She had to call over a Manager who finally figured out that the shelf price of $5 was THEIR mistake, but they had to honor that price. I am sure it got fixed quickly! Another time my wife was looking over her Walmart slip and noticed the Almond Flour was scanned twice so over charging her by $12. Yes, $15 or $12 is small potatoes, but many small potatoes add up over the long run. Watch your sales slips, bills, etc. to make sure your money is not being given to others incorrectly.

44. Phone calls to a company to dispute a charge or ask about a deal can sometimes be profitable.

Sometimes calling a company and disputing a charge or asking about how you can make your business with them be better can make you money. You might be put on hold and waste a lot of your time, but one time I got a free IPhone because I was willing to wait 45 minutes on the phone to dispute something. Don't be afraid to speak with a manager also. They seem to have more power to negotiate deals.

I once got a late mortgage charge on my house payment, so I called from Texas to the mortgage company in New Hampshire and asked for a one time forgiveness since I had never been late before. The guy on the phone looked at my account, saw that he was from a little town near me in South Texas and said,

"Don't worry about the charge and have a nice day!!!" Cool!

It seems I am forever calling my health insurance to dispute claims they don't pay. They have also made $800 billing mistakes and I had to find it and call them to get it fixed.

One time my daughter got a prescription from her doctor that cost $1200 when she went to pick it up at the pharmacy. Rather than just accepting the cost and paying it, she called her doctor and asked if there was anything they could help with. The doctor's office made some phone calls and sent my daughter to another pharmacy a little further away from her home, but the total cost of her medicine ended up being $20!!!! Not $1200! By not just blindly accepting the first bill she saved herself $1180!!!!!! That's huge! Great job Baby!

45. People like to talk, so be a good listener. I always say "never miss a good opportunity to shut-up" and "you will never learn anything with your mouth open".

I have a unique collection! I can say "Shut-up" in thirty different languages. I learned them from all the foreign students I got to teach over the years. That being said (and I realize I am saying a lot in this book), people like to talk. Too much in my opinion! They like to hear about themselves and not others. Or they like to brag or "one-up" your story. Don't be that person. Quite often it is hard to just sit there and listen, but think about how you feel about that person when they are going on and on. Usually it is best to keep to yourself. Be the bigger person. People like to be heard, so if you want to be around those kind of people, be a good listener. You can learn a lot by just listening!

46. A day you don't laugh is a day you don't live.

This was my senior year (Class of 79) quote. I try to have fun in everything I do. My brothers and I use to sing while scooping pig manure out of the barn. We also used to dive on and wrestle with hay bales as we picked them up out of the fields. It made a hot and hard job fun and made the time go faster! Even when teaching physics I tried to make it fun. I demonstrated things with toys and had some unique and fun things in class like having students put "Physics Baby" on everything they ever turned in for grading for the possibility of extra points.

Don't be afraid to laugh at yourself too. If you mess up or someone teases you about something, don't get all butt-hurt. Just have a laugh and move on. Don't take yourself too seriously!

47. Gentlemen, act like a gentleman!
Ladies, act like a lady!

I am a big believer in this one. I want my wife to be proud of me when we are out in public or even in our house and likewise I want to be proud of her. Guys...open doors for ladies and be polite. Be well dressed and well groomed! Nothing will impress a lady more than proper manners and grooming. Act like a gentleman! This doesn't stop once you are a couple either. We are 32 years into our marriage, and I still open doors for my wife.

Ladies, this works both ways! Look and act like a lady for your significant other. Some ladies are just more classy than others and this is due to how they act and the way they look. Notice I said "classy", not slutty. Yes I know makeup is a hassle, doing your hair takes forever, and good cloths can be expensive, but these are things that can impress a gentleman.

48. From what I have seen, for the most part, good things happen to good people and bad things happen to bad people, but unfortunately sometimes bad things happen to good people and good things sometimes happen to bad people.

You make your own luck in my opinion. If you are what is considered by society to be a "good" person normally "good" things will happen to you because you are around other "good" people and doing "good" things. Likewise, if you do "bad" things or hang around "bad" people the chances of "bad" things happening to you will increase. Not a lot of people get arrested at church.

The flip side of this goes along with #35. Sometimes Life Happens! Sometimes bad things do happen to good people and good things happen to bad people. That's just the way it goes, but if you are going to go with the averages, I'd rather try to be a good person.

49. Celebrate other people's successes. Be humble on your own.

When people around you have successes in life, be

genuinely happy for them and tell them so. Good Job! Congratulations! Way to go! Don't compare it to something you did or tell them about your successes! Let them have their moment!

Likewise be humble in your successes. Don't brag, don't advertise it everywhere. Just smile and know that your hard work has paid off.

50. Go on dates with your spouse.

I like this one. It goes along with #9. When you consider about 50% of all first marriages end in divorce and the divorce rates for 2nd and 3rd marriages is even higher, marriage must be tough! My wife and I have been married 32 years and we have fun every day.   A great marriage is amazing. It is like getting to live with your best friend. There is no one I would rather be with than my wife, but life gets busy when you are a grown up. Jobs, kids, commitments, and even the fun stuff all get in the way and unfortunately, we figure our marriage is an automatic or a "given", so it sometimes gets the least attention. Wrong!!!   Keep falling in love! Go on dates, buy flowers, kiss every day in the morning and evening, and say "I love you" every day!

51. Be responsible for your own mistakes. Don't blame others, and don't wait for a handout or "bailout".

If you screw up or make a mistake, own up to it. Some mistakes are worse than others. Hopefully it will not hurt you too much, but if it does it will help you learn not to do it again. Also, don't throw the blame on others if it is your fault. Too many bosses will blame their employees, not themselves. They throw the employees under the bus to cover their mistakes and that is not right.

There is also no such thing as a free meal.. It might be free for you, but somebody is paying for it. If you go bankrupt, default on a loan, or get a government entitlement, someone is paying for. Rather than standing there with your hand out, use that hand to work and earn some money.

52. I have noticed that the more mentally positive you are, the less physically sick you get.

I am sure if there is some sort of medical research out about this subject, but this goes along with #17 and having a positive attitude. I feel that if you want to be sick, you can mentally make yourself sick. On the other side of that if you have a positive mentality, I believe you will not get sick as often.

I only called in sick twice in my twenty-eight year career as a teacher when I was actually sick. I'm talking stuff coming out of the north and south ends at the same time! Not fun. Oh sure, I did call in sick for special appointments or to go to our daughters' school programs, but that was like a "mental day". If you do get sick you still need to have a positive attitude to recover. Take care of yourself and get better. On the other hand don't be that guy that goes to work sick and gets everyone else sick. Nobody likes that guy.

53. Get reservations if you know what you are doing. It saves time.

Most decent restaurants these days will take reservations. If you are sure about when and where you are going out to eat either call the restaurant or check out their website to see if you can make online reservations. Sometimes this can save you a lot of time sitting around the door of the place or the bar waiting for a table to open. It impresses a date too!!! This works for some movie theaters now too.

54. Be involved in your children's lives.

There are so many ways to be involved in your children's lives. Be their little league coach, their Girl Scout leader, a school volunteer, their Sunday school teacher, or a million other things. You don't have to be perfect at the job, just be there! I didn't know anything about coaching a little girls soccer team, but the 11 seasons my girls and I had together went by in a flash and I would do it all again in a minute. There will come a time when they are not around and you wish they were so enjoy the time you have! You will have plenty of time in your life later on to sit in your big chair and watch TV or surf the internet, (or write a book).

55. Eat healthy while you are young and develop the habit because the older you get the slower you and your metabolism gets and it gets hard to maintain a healthy weight.

So easy to say, so difficult to do. When I was young I could eat and drink anything I wanted and not gain a pound. Now it seems like I am fighting my weight all the time. Every phase I go through (high school, college, married, retired) my weight shifts up. Just try to be mindful of your weight and health not obsessed.

Once again Life Happens and sometimes our health is what gets put on the side burner due to all the other "important" things. Jobs, family, career are all very important, but your health?!?! In my mind I think it would be easier to not gain weight than it is to try and lose weight.

56. People die. Again...I'm sorry.

This one truly sucks, but death is a part of life. I am 100% sure that I will die someday. It hurts!!! If you love that person that dies it feels like someone has punched you as hard as they can in your gut and ripped your heart out. I truly hate it, but it is impossible to avoid. You have to do your best to suck it up and move on knowing that the loved one who passed away would want you to carry on and make them proud. I have had a lot of people I loved pass away and there are many more to go and I am really not looking forward to it. It is a really tough part of life! Good Luck!

57. Learn to swim even if you are getting older.

I am a pool rat so this has never been an issue with me or my family, but I have met many adults that for one reason or another cannot swim. Learn!!! You don't have to swim the English Channel, but try to get over your fear of water and be comfortable in a pool, so you can get in with your children or grandchildren.

58. Buying things online has its pros and cons.

People do a lot of shopping on the internet. I do a lot of shopping on the internet too. I see both sides of the story here. Sometimes things are cheaper on the internet. A huge amount?? That depends on what you are buying and if you have to pay sales tax or not. We live in a pretty remote area where there are not too many retail stores around, so often we can get things delivered to our house quicker and cheaper than if we had to drive to the city to find it. When we did live by a city, I often could buy things online and maybe get it cheaper, but avoid the local 8.25% sales tax added on to the price. On a $1000 item that adds up.

On negative side of online shopping is that the online stores you are buying from do NOT support the local community activities the way your local businesses do. Amazon will not buy jerseys for your daughter's soccer team, but a local restaurant will. If you don't support your local stores they may not be around too long, and that hurts your town in many ways. The less amount of money that stays in your town means fewer businesses, fewer jobs, less taxes, and soon the town will get smaller and die.

59. Some of the best investments you can make are in your health and education.

Quite often spending some money on your education or training for your job is a good thing. The more skills you have that differentiate you from others, the more job opportunities and/or job security you will have.

Likewise you should invest in your health too. We have one body that needs to lasts us our lifetime. Take care of yourself. I know things happen that are out of our control, but there are a lot of things we can easily do or NOT do to help us live healthier lives. Stay active, avoid smoking, eat sensibly.

60. Education is great, but avoid college loans.

As I said earlier you don't need a college education, but you might want to have some talent or skill that people are willing to pay you for. College can be VERY expensive, and I am amazed how much money banks will loan an 18 year old with no job!! Books alone can run you $500/semester which is ridiculous. Be very careful! There are private schools, state schools, and community schools. All are very different in price, but all are very good for getting an education. Be careful about getting into college debt. Did you know that the only way get out of your college loans is to either pay it off or die. No bankruptcy or defaulting. I have even read about people who are approaching retirement and STILL paying for their college loans. Even worse is parents cosigning for a child's college loans and getting stuck with them.

61. Do the things you <u>have</u> to do now, so you can do the things you <u>want</u> to do later.

It's called paying your dues! You probably won't get your dream job right away in your career (or you may never get it), but chances are good that your first job will be tough. It is at this point of your life you need to put in the time and work hard. Pay your dues. Be the first one there and the last one to leave. Do what needs to be done. Get the education. Get the training. Get the skills. Do things now while you have the time because life is going to happen and you want to be prepared.

62. Truly good friends are very rare and very hard to find.

Some people make friends easy. I'm not that guy. I figure if you have 2 or 3 REALLY good friends at once in your life, you are doing pretty good. The kind who will get up in the middle of the snowy night and come help you pull your car out of a ditch. The real "Go To" people. They are rare! Most of the friends you have are what I call "superficial". They are friends and good people by acquaintance or work, but not the "true" friends. These kind of friends come and go with different phases of your life, but some of them remain true friends.

63. Be trustworthy and a person of your word.

This one speaks volumes about you. Be dependable, be honest, keep your word, and follow through with your actions. I don't care who you are, what you do, or how much you earn, ALWAYS keep your word. If people can't trust you, it will hurt your reputation. I don't mean physically hurt, but from a personal point people will shy away from you both in friendships and the workplace and those relationships will not grow as they should.

64. Always teach as if your own child is in the room.

When I was a teacher I taught with a sarcastic yet humorous tone. Yes, I picked on kids playfully, but I never tried to hurt anyone. One day a student asked me if I would teach that way if my daughter was in my classroom. Very good question! It made me think, but I answered yes because I was trying to take a very difficult subject (Physics) and make it fun. After that I consciously taught as if my daughters were in my classroom. I believe if you do the best for your child you will give your best for other kids too! This goes not just for the classroom, but for anywhere. You might be a coach, working in a store, or just being around kids, but as an adult, young people are looking at you all the time and learning from you whether you want them to or not. Be a good adult role model.

65. Don't go into too much debt for a car. It is just a car!

In this day and age this lesson is very tough and I can't say I have always followed it always because I have done some car loans in my time, but be careful here. Car dealerships make is VERY easy to buy cars. 0% down, 0% Interest), bad credit, no credit, no JOB!?!?!?

You name it and they will loan you money. Of course the worse risk you are not to repay the loan the higher the interest rate you pay, but they don't talk too much about that. They will even let you finance a car for 96 months!!! THAT IS 8 YEARS PEOPLE!!!! Crazy!!! If you need to take a car loan, get it for 3 years. If you can't afford those terms you are buying a car you either can't afford or don't deserve. Not only have I never had a car loan go full term, in other words I pay them off early, but I once kept a pick-up for 19 years!!!!   It was a real POS (piece of #@%&), but I called it my $100,000 truck because that's how much money I figured I saved by paying it off early and driving it that long. I loved that truck.

66. Be respectful of others.

Being respectful just means being nice. If you don't know a person then give them the benefit of the doubt and show them respect. Saying things like Yes Sir, Yes Ma'am, Please, and Thank you REALLY go a long ways. Some people may lose my respect eventually because of their words or actions, but for the most part I try to show respect to people.

67. If you are going to have children, be sure you can raise and support them

Being a parent is the BEST thing I ever did! If you are going to have children be ready to give them your time, your love, and your money.   Do not expect other people or the government to pay for or take care of your children. They are your children!!! You raise them and you pay for them! Why should others??? I know this will not be a popular lesson, but we know what causes babies so if you are not ready for the time and expense of children...don't have them. I am not saying you have to be abstinent, but don't get pregnant if you are not ready. Likewise don't expect your parents or in-laws to be free babysitters ALL THE TIME! They are grandparents and they love your children, but they have earned their dues (and rest) when they raised you. They don't have to start all over again if they don't want to. YES...some grandparents want to. That's fine if it is truly their choice. That being said I will almost always be available to my daughters if they need me.

68. Figure out what your gift or gifts are in life is and try to make a living doing it.

We all have "gifts" in life. Things that we are good at that seem to come easy to us, but not to all people. If you can figure out what your gifts are and use them to earn a living, you will be blessed. I stumbled into mine. I don't like being in front of people, but when I became a teacher I learned I was pretty good at teaching physics and ended up really enjoying my career. Maybe it's languages, computers, or whatever your skill may be if you are lucky enough to earn a living with that gift you will enjoy your career a whole lot more.

69. Be honest with people and don't talk behind their back.

A. You should always be honest and tell the truth. It just makes things easier and people will trust you more.

B. Talking behind someone's back isn't very nice. Usually when you do this it is pure gossip and almost always negative towards the other person. Negativity breeds negativity and you could end up hurting someone.

70. Learn to whistle loud. It is a nice tool for emergencies.

I forget when I learned this "skill", but I can stick 2 fingers in my mouth and whistle very loudly. VERY LOUD! The best I have been measured at is 123 db which is above the pain threshold of humans.   The main way I used this "skill" was to call my daughters when I didn't know where they were. People have kidded me that my daughters are trained on a whistle like dogs, but their whole childhood all I had to do was whistle and they knew to come running. Whether they were riding their bikes around the neighborhood, out exploring while we were camping, or even if I lost sight of them in a Walmart, all I had to do was whistle and they came running. It was very much a safety thing for us. Later as a teacher I also learned it was a very effective way to get my students to quiet down too.

71. Live Your Life!

This lesson actually has 2 meanings. First of all, live your life and NOT someone else's life. With social media and television being as big and popular as they are today it is real ease to get wrapped up in the life of other people and not your own. It's ok to keep in contact with people and all, but when you are spending too much time checking their posts and status it kind of wastes your own life.

The second part of this is making sure you LIVE your life! How sad would it be to wake up someday when you are old and realize all you did for your whole life was get up, go to work, go home, repeat for 40 or 50 years, and then wait to die. I'm not real good at sitting around most of the time. I like to keep moving. I think I was ADHD before it was cool.

72. Always kiss and say "I love you" to your spouse before you leave the house in the morning and before you go to sleep at night.

You never know what is going to happen during a day. Like I said earlier, "Life Happens". If something does happen you don't want your last conversation with your loved one being about not picking up your underwear or something else not important. Likewise never go to sleep mad at each other. You won't sleep that good in the first place, but the argument , for better or worse, will still be there in the morning.

73.Remember your P's and Q's.

Always say **P**lease and Thank you! Thank-**Q**!! Get it!?!? Anyway, this is one that probably most parents have said in one form or another. Good manner are very important in getting along with people and it seems in this day and age it is a lost art. The best way to get people to like you, be nice to you, work hard for you, give you good service, and/or buy from you is to have good manners.

With that being said the main person you should have proper manners for is your spouse. Just because you live with them and/or have been married to them for many years doesn't mean you can't be nice to them Even for the little stuff that you see everyday...say please and thank you!

74. Have good attendance at school and your job! You will learn more and get fired less.

This is one of the lessons I didn't understand until I was older and in the working world. You get paid to do your job! Yes, I know some of you think school doesn't "pay" you, but many studies prove that an education of any kind is directly related to making a better income. Anyway, good attendance at either school or your job is very important. Good bosses and teachers notice these things too and will reward you for it in some way. I know things happen and you do need to miss, but those are the times you really need to use your days. Another thing I did notice on my job was on those days I was gone it seemed like I had to work harder planning for the absence and "cleaning up" after the absence than if I had actually been there. It is also called "having a good work ethic"!

75. Always wear your seatbelt.

Back in the "old days" it was not the law to wear seat belts so we didn't. I personally was in a wreck one time and hit the dash of my truck with my head going 60 mph. Eight stitches and a concussion later I learned where my seatbelt was and how to wear it. Maybe physics or death statistics didn't exist back then or maybe we were just dumb, but now it just makes sense to wear your seat belt and it is the law. Seat belts save lives! Airbags save lives! Also the law says wear it properly. One time my wife got pulled over by a policeman because he saw that my daughter did not have the seat belt shoulder strap over her shoulder. She was short and wore it under her arm so it didn't rub on her neck. Well...one ticket for "not wearing it properly" and a $200 fine later she learned.

76. When you are at a STOP light and it turns green... Don't go!!! Look both ways again and then go.

People are always in a hurry and trying to beat the yellow lights in the cities. It seems like Red means STOP, Green means GO, and Yellow means GO LIKE HELL! This is just scary because if you go on a green and they run through their light they will T-bone your car. Yes, they will be at fault for the police report and insurance, but you are going to be the one in the

77. Sometimes you need to spend money to save or make money.

We had an air conditioner on our home that was 17 years old and ran all the time in hot weather which gave us very high electric bills. After looking around I priced one for around $5000. I hated spending that kind of money to replace an AC that was working, but it was super inefficient and wasting money. After we replaced it, our electric bill dropped $200+ a month which quickly helped pay for the new AC.

Another example is switching our lights to LED bulbs. The upfront cost is more, but it will save money in the long run both in bulb replacement and electricity.

78. Don't get distracted while driving.

This is so easy to do now that we have cell phones with everything from music to GPS in them. Some cars even have WIFI included. Tell me that's not stupid. And it is not just your phone! It is your radio, the scenery, your friends, or anything that takes your eyes off the road in front of you. I just about rear-ended a car once while I was clipping a fingernail. Stupid!!! And one time I was rear ended by a lady putting on her makeup while driving. Stupid!!!!

At the speed of 55 mph if you read a text for 5 seconds you have traveled the length of a football field and not looked at the road. We all think we can do this, but in reality it is very dangerous.

79. Be very careful about trusting people you work with. You can get stabbed in the back real quick.

You need to trust the people you work with. It is very important in a job environment, but be careful who you trust. Some people are just out for themselves and will hurt you and others if it helps get them ahead in the workplace or look good in front of the boss.

80. Don't gossip!

It is so easy to gossip about people behind their backs and fun too. Everyone does it, but that doesn't mean it is right. Usually gossip is hurting someone, and they are not there to defend themselves or their actions. It also can come back to bite you in the butt if that person finds out it was you who was spreading the gossip. If you can't say something nice, don't say anything at all.

81. Get a flu shot and other immunizations as needed.

Through the advancements of modern medicine there are many illnesses we can prevent now with vaccines.
We all received many of these vaccinations when we were babies. The Influenza or flu is the most common vaccination needed on a yearly basis, but many people are such babies!! I always hear people saying "the flu shot made me sick once!! " Bull!! It is dead virus they give you. Maybe they got a little sick from it OR they were already infected when they got the shot, but the flu virus does NOT give you the flu. The flu shot is only for the most popular flu strains that particular season so it is not 100% for sure you won't get the flu, but get the shot! "But I don't like shots...they hurt!" Grow up, suck it up, and be tough. There are many other immunizations that are helpful and people have concerns with them so you will have to do your own research and come to your own conclusions, but I am a believer in immunizations. I just got a vaccination for shingles this week. My arm hurt for 3 days, but it is a lot better than getting the shingles I have been told.

82. Get a wellness screening and blood test once a year.

This is simple to do and often these things come with your insurance for low or no cost if you are blessed enough to have a job with health insurance. After all the insurance companies want you to be healthy, so they don't have to pay out more when you get sick. Even if you don't have insurance many hospitals will do this monthly for a smaller fee. A quick doctor visit for blood pressure and blood screenings can tell a lot about your health and can many times catch things before they get too advanced.

83. Don't be afraid to donate blood.

This is a good thing. It helps a lot of people and doesn't cost you anything but time and a little pain, just a tiny pin prick in the arm. It's really not bad at all! Also, you never know if you or a loved one will be the one who needs blood and you hope there is some blood available so please get out there and help people.

84. If you are interested in someone as far as dating or more, look at what they do, not what they say.

In other words actions speak louder than words. When someone is trying to impress another person it is so easy to build themselves up by "stretching the truth" a bit. We all do it I suppose, but some take it to the extremes. Look at what they do or their actions in life. Are they nice or rude, loud or soft, kind or mean, self-centered or caring, healthy or not, and the list goes on and on, but watch them. Do they open doors for you? Do they say please and thank you? Watch their actions and how they live. That is how they really are.

85. Making your bed every day in the morning must be a good thing because my wife and mother do it.

I confess that I am not a bed maker. For me it is a waste of time, or I am just lazy, but research shows that you are more likely to become a millionaire or successful if you make your bed every day. Not because someone is going to pay you, but because you are accomplishing a goal the very first thing of the day, and it get you going on a positive trend to accomplish more positive things that day.

86. Start saving for your retirement as soon as possible.

When it comes to saving for retirement, your mindset should be the sooner the better. Use time to your advantage while you are young and make Compound Interest your friend. Roth IRA's are an amazing investment tool to beat taxes for long term investments especially for young people and if they qualify. If not a Roth IRA start a regular IRA, or a 401k, or a 403b. As long as the money is invested in a tax sheltered account and you can't use it until you are 59 ½ years old. If you do use it early you have to pay a 10% penalty to the government along with any income taxes you have to declare. Paying off debt before you invest for your retirement it important too. It doesn't make sense to pay interest on money you owe **and** get interest of money saved. Usually the debt interest you pay will be much more than the savings interest you earn.

87. Start saving for your children's college as soon as they are born.

Once again try to use time to your advantage. You have about 18 years to save for their college. We started each of our kids 529 college savings plans with $1000 and then added between $100 to $200 per month until they went to college.   Both of our kids went to state colleges and we paid cash for it.   They did get some scholarships which was nice, but the majority we paid for.   While I don't recommend it, kids can take loans for college, but parents can't take a loan for retirement so have your saving priorities straight.

88. Talk to your children every day about how their day was and then LISTEN. Don't judge.

Kids will talk to you about "things" if you don't judge them immediately or get too preachy.   Ask them how their day was and listen to what they have to say. You might be amazed at what is going on it their lives and how it helps your relationship with them as they grow up.

89. Listen to the little voice in your head.

This is called intuition and it seems to work. Through evolution we have developed an instinct or gut reaction that helps us survive. We need to listen to it more often. Usually the difference between right and wrong, good and bad, or safe and stupid is obvious and our evolutionary intuition tries to steer us in the right direction, but our brain and ego sometimes overrules it, and we choose the wrong option. Many times it is best to go with your first or gut reaction.

90. If something does not feel right, remove yourself from the situation.

Very similar to intuition are the little hairs on the back of your neck. If you know you are in some situation that is wrong or being somewhere is wrong...get out of there! I always told my girls they could blame me for anything to other people, but if they ever found themselves in a bad place or a bad situation they could call me anytime and I would come get them with no questions asked (until the morning).

91. One of the hardest parts about being a parent is coming home after a long, hard day at work and playing football or Barbie.

When you get home from work it just feels good to grab the TV remote and relax. But what about your kids who have more energy than you??? It is way too easy to drop them in front of the TV too, but as tired as

you are, engage with your kids. Play Barbie, kick a
soccer ball, throw a football, swim, or just go for a bike
ride. There is plenty of time for TV later in life. Your
kids are going to grow up fast.

92. Never allow a man hurt you.

Never allow a man to hurt you physically, mentally, or
emotionally. All are equally damaging, but please know
you do NOT have to put up with any kind of pain or
abuse from anyone. You do NOT deserve it!

93. If a relationship is rocky already, getting married or having a child will not help the situation.

Marriage and/or children will NOT save a
relationship most of the time! It does however add
stress to a relationship which will make an already
difficult situation harder. Whether it is emotional stress,
time stress, or financial stress it really doesn't matter
because it is all stress. Take your time.

94. Smoking is bad!

There is way too much data out there to ignore this. Thirty percent of all cancer is related to smoking. You can Google it yourself. That is like pointing a 6 cylinder gun at your head with 2 out of the 6 chambers loaded with bullets! My father died at age 69...he smoked. My father-in-law died at age 67...he smoked. Both had quit later in their lives, but the damage was done. And don't tell me vaping is a better alternative because it is not! Look it up! Both smoking and vaping curb your appetite so you are thinner, or it's a habit that is hard to break, but it is killing you.

95. Never compare your children.

Love your children for who they are! Try not to compare them to other siblings or other kids their age. Just because one kid is good at something doesn't mean another kid will be good at that same thing. As a parent I felt it was my job to expose my daughters to many things and see what they enjoyed. Maybe they will...maybe they won't, but you can't fit a round peg into a square hole. Hopefully they will find their "thing" someday and run with it!

96. When you turn 50 years old get a colonoscopy.

Colon cancer is one of the very preventable cancers. You just need to start getting colonoscopies at the age of 50. Sooner if you have a family history of colon cancer or polyps. Are they fun? Not really, but not that bad. Do they hurt? NO! Are they cheap? Depends on your insurance, but could cost you a $1000 or so, but what is your life worth? Don't give me that macho crap and say, "I ain't paying no doctor to stick a camera up my butt," because if you are dying of cancer nobody is macho. My father-in-law retired in December and found he had colon cancer (because he had blood in his poop) in January. Two years of chemo, which is not a great quality of life, and he passed away. He was a good man, but just hadn't thought to have the colonoscopy yet. Ask your doctor!

97. Don't believe everything you hear, see, or read especially on the Internet.

In today's world of computers and with the Internet and social media you simply cannot believe everything you hear, see, or read. Rumors run rampant, pictures are altered, and yes… people lie! Don't be a sucker and fall for everything.

98. K.I.S.S. (Keep it Simple Stupid)

This are words I live by and I find applies in so many places or situations. Don't over think a situation or make it more difficult or complex than it is. Many times the simple solution is the right solution. I had a boss tell me once "there is an easy way and a hard way to do everything. Take a little extra time and figure out the easy way."

99. In college study in a field and get extra skills that will help you get a job. Many times those extra skills will help you get the job.

The first job out of college is the hardest to get because employers don't know what skills you have or the work ethic you have that can help their company. Hopefully your degree will help them know your skill set, but also try to develop different skills that will make you a better candidate for the job.

100. You should "never judge a book by its cover," but "first impressions are important."

I saw this time and time again as a teacher. A kid would walk into the room the first day and I would form a first impression about them due to their appearance. Maybe they dressed different, maybe they had colored hair, dressed preppy, or maybe piercings, or tattoos. Either way it is hard not to form an opinion. Sometimes I was right and many times I was wrong. That big kid dressed in all black baggy clothes, slouched shoulders, messy hair, and had a bad body odor was one of the nicest kids I ever taught. When he failed my class I told him "you are the nicest kid to ever fail my class" to which he replied "yes sir. I didn't work as hard as I should have!" He totally owned it and that gained my respect.

While I agree that you can't judge a book by its cover, I am also not going to pick up the book and buy it if the cover does not appeal to me. In other words, some jobs want you to look a certain way for the job. What that look is depends on the job, but if you don't have the look that they want, chances are you will not get the job when you interview.

101. Fix the problem.

This was and is the "go to" phrase I always said to my
daughters and students when they would come to me or
call me with a problem. I was more than willing to help,
but they won't learn if I enable them by telling them
how to do something or fixing it for them. Do what
needs to be done to fix the problem! Don't lie, cheat,
or steal, but think about what needs to be done and do
it! It might take some long phone calls, you might have
to go somewhere, you might not like what you have to
do, but the problem needs fixing so fix it!

102. Save money where you can.

I love talking to some of my older friends and
relatives about saving money because they really know
what it is like to not have any. Especially if they were
alive at the Great Depression of 1929. Many of these
people remember what it is like to be poor growing up
and have nothing. Literally nothing. Having this
attitude about money is not a bad thing. It is too easy
to blow money. Our society is always pressuring us to
spend what we have, but we need to try and look down
the financial road and save where we can. One time a
student of mine, who worked at the local grocery store,
was going to bring some food for an orphanage my
classes supports. I mentioned that as an employee he

probably got a discount to which he said "yes, but it is only 8%." I then told him if I could get a guaranteed 8% return on my investments I would put all my money in it. Another student and I were walking down the hallway one day and I stopped to pick up a penny on the floor. He said "Coach, you pick up pennies???" to which I said "every penny I pick up is one step closer to two million dollars!" He got the message!

103. Chances are good you won't like your first job, but that's ok!

I hated my first job! With a college degree in hand I got a whole $3.75/hour and no extra for overtime. One week I clocked in 111 hours. Yes that is almost 16 hours a day for 4 weeks. Hated it and only stayed there 9 months. On the bright side that job did teach me how to work hard and it gave me experience I needed to find a much better job. I didn't particularly care for that job either, but stayed there 18 months before I totally rebooted my life and took another employment direction where I found my calling!

104. Learn to use a plunger on a clogged toilet before it is needed.

This seems like a dumb lesson, but as my daughter found out in her college dorm room, when a toilet is overflowing on the floor it is NOT a good time to learn how to plunge a toilet. Just a little practice on clean water will give you loads of confidence when an emergency happens. Never hurts to know where the plunger is also.

105. It never hurts to have a side job for a little extra income if you need it, especially when you are young and energetic.

There is an old saying that says "make hay while the sun is shining." When you are young and have more time before the children come into your life, this is a good time to do a side job to either pay off debt or get ahead financially. You can also use this money to invest because it is never too early to invest.

106. Everyone in your family is more important than anyone online or your status.

This is a sign of the times, but not necessarily a good sign. Put down or turn off the damn phone! I know we all have jobs and we think we are important, but not as important as spending quality time with your family. Make your dinner table a "no phone zone." There are also many more important and productive things you can do with your free time than play Minecraft or checking your Instagram. I'm not saying quit playing them altogether, but there is a time and place for that kind of entertainment. Don't ignore people for your phone.

107. Just because something is different, does not mean it is bad.

Just because someone or something is different from what we know or are use to does not mean it is wrong or bad. We need to keep an open mind when it comes to things that are not familiar to us. It might be a different culture or way of thinking, but just because we don't agree with it that does not make it wrong or bad.

108. If your marriage has a parent staying home to raise the kids you still need a financial plan.

Having you or your spouse stay at home to raise the children is an amazing gift for the children and a family, but you still need to have a financial plan for retirement in place for the person staying home in case something should happen. Layoffs, disability, divorce, etc. The at home parent should also have some sort of retirement plan going just in case.

109. Change the filters around you.

This kind of goes with #18. There are many hidden filter in our lives we need to know about and remember to change as needed. Not just the oil filter in a car, but the air conditioner in our home or apartment, the air filter in our car engine, gas filters, refrigerator water, etc. These filters clean the air or liquid going through it thereby saving wear and tear on that machine. BUT if you don't change a dirty filter it restricts flow through the product and causes the machine to work too hard. Check your filters! An air conditioner filter should be changes every 1 to 3 months.

110. Dress in layers.

If you live it a place that has dramatic weather swings (like Iowa) always dress in layers. Have a big outer layer that is waterproof and then multiple layers of insulation (fleece or wool) underneath. My theory is you can always take cloths off, but if you don't have them you can't put them on.

111. Never hit a lady.

This is wrong!!. Boys do NOT hit girls and gentlemen do NOT hit ladies. Period. Exclamation!

112. "Happy wife, happy life" is so true, but better yet Happy spouse, happy house."

I love my wife to the moon and back and will do anything for her, but we both know this door swings both ways. Both partners in a relationship need to be happy and have their needs met in order for a marriage to truly prosper.

113. The sun always shines! It might be night time or covered by a cloud, but it always shines.

This has a deeper meaning. What it means is that sometimes things go bad and it makes life miserable, but those times don't last. They are just a blip on the radar of life. Focus on the good in your life because it will be back. A friend of mine said "in 20 years this will just be a sentence." I like that! "My dog died, I got laid-off, the kids were horrible today." Later on it's just a memory and things got better because the sun always shines!

Later on in my career I thought to myself that maybe my students would have some Life Lessons of their own. I asked them to write down some things that they had learned and experienced in their young lives.

Not surprisingly I got pure gold! Because they are not mine, there are no stories involved so you can read into it what you want.

Life Lesson from Teenagers for Teenagers

- The most beautiful things tend to be the simplest.
- Get up early! It is always good to have extra time to do things instead of rushing.
- When filling the tank with gas use the slowest speed. It takes more time, but it lessens the amount lost to escaping vapor fumes.
- Stupid says "Yes", Smart says "No".
- Listen to your parent's advice. It can save you from a lot of trouble.
- "Love like crazy". I have learned that sharing acts of love can change people's life. It's also a universal language.
- Don't mess around in class. It is easier if you listen and do your work.
- If something doesn't go your way… move on!

- Figuring out what you do with your life is only half the equation. More importantly, I believe it's who you're with when you are doing it.
- Don't always follow your heart because in the end it is not always the best.
- Follow your head even if it hurts because you start to realize how people really treat you.
- Never take a drink from someone at a party, no matter how nice they are.
- Live your life while you are young. Kids want to grow up too fast and adults want to be kids again.
- God gives us a body as a gift. Why ruin it with tattoos and piercings?
- Guys and especially girls... using profanity doesn't make you anymore ATTRACTIVE.
- You can make everything fun, you just don't want to all the time.
- You will never know how much impact you will cause in a person's life or how much they will impact you.
- Life is like a puzzle, each person in your life completes you in some sort of way.
- Take a photography class. It helps you see the beauty of things.

- Don't stress about helping people from other places when your own neighbor is in need.
- Every life has a purpose; it can be to start or to end something, but this doesn't mean you have to do both.
- Get some sun.
- Make a habit to do work.
- Making plans is good, but sometimes it's better to take action.
- Always have someone that knows where you are. It might come in handy at some point.
- Look forward for little changes in your life every once in a while.
- Try by yourself first and if that doesn't work then ask for help.
- Enjoy the little things.
- Always be a gentleman or lady and keep your morals.
- Sing Hakuna Mattata when you are having trouble.
- You can act stupid, but never do stupid things.
- Work hard today and you can live easy tomorrow. If you work easy today, you will live hard tomorrow.

- When you get older, remember that your family's happiness is priority #1, but that doesn't mean you have to be rich and give them everything they want. It means being together, enjoying life, and keeping them safe.

- Give yourself a break when it is needed, not wanted.
- It really doesn't matter that you got to the top of the mountain, it is how you got there that does.
- Start saving as soon as possible. You never know when a little extra cash will be needed.
- Don't fully trust the bank. Their job is to handle money. Don't let them handle you.
- If you don't have a good memory give yourself notes (or use your phone) to remind you of upcoming things. This is better than having to tell someone that you forgot their special event.
- Keep your house clean and help your parents with chores.
- Live in the present, not the past.
- Learn to play an instrument or sing. You will view the world differently.
- Do the things you have to do now so you don't pay for them later.

- Never post something on the internet (Facebook, Instagram, Twitter) that you don't want people (parents) to see.
- Always tell your parents who you are with and where you are. Also, call them when you arrive to where you are going. They will learn to trust you more.
- No matter what collision you are going through in life, always remember something better is coming after the collision.
- Practice driving before you take driver's education class. The instructor will yell less.
- Even if you don't understand the assignment or finish the homework, turn something in. It does help.
- Don't lose confidence in yourself.
- If you have a talent or gift...don't waste it.
- Life is a marathon not a sprint, so enjoy the run.
- Never let anyone change the way you are.
- Don't do something to someone if you wouldn't want them to do it to you.
- Buy a PillowPet.
- Hard work and dedication are great, but don't obsess over it to the point you get sick. Everything in moderation.

- Remember to be a kid while you are young.
- Don't procrastinate! It causes too much stress later.
- Don't be afraid to try new things, you never know what can happen.
- Be nice to your brothers and sisters. They can be your best friends later in life.
- Don't hold grudges against family and friends. You never know when you might need their help.
- Don't burn your bridges as you cross them. People come and go in your life and you might see them again.
- Hard work does pay off.
- Challenge yourself and don't settle for less.
- Never underestimate how thirsty you can get... be prepared.
- Always be honest with yourself.
- Don't hang around with manipulative people if you can avoid it.
- Not everyone is going to like you...deal with it!
- Never give people a reason to think of you differently than the person you really are.
- Always be true to yourself. Honesty is your best policy.

- People may be mad at you for your mistakes, but they will respect you for admitting them.
- Try to be more understanding so you will be less ignorant later.
- We are in no position to judge anyone, but we can learn from them
- When you are stuck in a bad situation, don't panic, it may kill you.
- Be sincere and set a positive example. You will be surprised at how much more approachable you will become.
- Don't procrastinate. It will help you later on in life.
- Develop good habits. (Reading, studying, etc.)
- Be interested in what is going on in your community, region, country, and the planet.
- The decisions you make now will affect you for the rest of your life. Make wise decisions.
- Don't give into peer pressure.

- When driving a friend, and they are persuading you to drive fast or perform an action that you know is bad, or will have negative consequences, DON'T DO IT!!! BE SMART!

- Don't beat yourself up if you fail a test. It happens.
- Girls, don't fall for a boy too easily.
- Boys, don't fall for a girl too easy.
- Looking presentable in the way you dress can tell people who don't truly know you a lot.
- The right thing to do isn't always the best thing to do and the best thing to do isn't always the right thing to do.
- Try new foods.
- If you are ever going to drop a deuce at school go to the locker room of the JROCT.
- Don't feel ashamed of being called a geek or nerd by other people. You most likely are going to become their boss.
- Never call a girl fat. You are bound to get slapped.
- Don't lose sight of your faith. When all else fails God will be there.
- When there's a food fight watch where you are running so you don't fall into the food.
- Sometimes fitting in isn't the best way to make friends, but make enemies.
- Always carry a sweater when you go to school.

- Take your charger with you wherever you go, you don't know what will happen and when your phone will be needed.
- Exercise, it helps everything.
- Buy fuzzy socks. They rock and take care of your feet. You also don't know what is on the floor.
- Try to not depend on others for things you can do by yourself.
- Try to stay away from people that are alcoholics and drug addicts.
- Family comes always comes first.
- Have a passion and do something you want, but not for the money, but because you love to do it.
- Live everyday of your life like it's your last.
- Say "I love you" to your parents every day.
- Enjoy the little things in life.
- Always have a backup major so you have something to fall back on.
- Don't take life for granted, but live it up to it's fullest.
- Don't take other people's choices for you. You choose your own route and stick with it.

- Always have a way to connect to people in case of emergencies: Cell phone, computer, etc.
- Save money!   Invest for yourself.
- Get check-ups yearly from your doctor. Stay healthy and be aware of what's happening in your body.
- At your most embarrassing moments in your life take pictures to be able to look back and laugh about your old embarrassing moments.
- Don't be afraid to not please anyone, because you can't please everyone.
- Don't let what others (followers) influence you or change your opinion. Do what's best for you and think about the consequences.
- Become friends with someone you normally wouldn't be friends with.
- Run every day.
- Enjoy high school! Leave relationships for after high school.
- Use your time wisely. Don't strain yourself. Use a planner to keep track of your schedule.
- Be your own person. Don't try to be what everyone else wants you to be.
- Plan ahead.   Try to take as many extra classes as you can.

- If they talk about others with you, they'll talk about you to others.   Choose friends wisely.
- A few good friends are better than a million bad ones.
- Tell those who you love that you love them. Tomorrow is not a promise.
- School first. Party later.
- Don't get a girlfriend or boyfriend until you get a career or a source of income.
- Try to buy a 4 cylinder car and make payments on time. Saves you gas!
- Try to learn different things like fixing something or building it.
- Even if you are not good in a school subject, it might help you later in life.
- When you are in school (middle school, high school), try to ride the bus. It saves your parents money instead of wasting gas. The school bus ride is free.
- Living isn't free falling, living is falling freely.
- Bringing someone else down won't make you happier, but being nice to people will.
- You get out of life what put into it.
- Always try to be a good person. It will pay off.
- If you believe something is unfair, express your opinion.

- Do not overstress about simple and stupid stuff.
- Think of all the consequences before acting.
- No boyfriend or girlfriend is worth losing your friendship with your best friends.
- Take school seriously. It only gets harder down the road.
- Don't always judge someone by their actions unless you put yourself in their shoes.
- If you and a good friend are no longer on "speaking terms", and you find out they're talking negative things about you, and you get angry or sad, it's most likely because you still miss the relationship you had with that one friend.
- Do whatever you need, despite what others say.
- If mess up socially in high school, forget it. You'll laugh about it when you're 25.
- Think for yourself before you think about others.
- Have multiple options, not just one.
- Don't look too far forward. Your life will skip by in a blink of an eye. Basically, enjoy every moment.

- Cherish the time with your family. You won't get to as much time with them after high school.
- Go to concerts. There's nothing like seeing your favorite band or artist live.
- Do more of what you love.
- No matter what happens don't let life keep you down. Keep moving forward.
- Always plan ahead.
- Save money now, watch it grow, and spend it later.
- You change and the people around you change. Learn to let go and move on because it's usually for the better.
- Always be open-minded.
- If you don't need it, don't buy it.
- Live life to the fullest because you can be gone the next day.
- Spend as much time as you can with family because in the end, memories are all you have.
- Your freshmen friends will change; then again so will all your friends every other year.
- You're going to date people in high school, just don't let them dictate it.

- Refrain from fighting with your parents and just talk it out. In a yelling match you'll just forget that your parents were once your age.
- Don't follow bad crowds. Do what's right. Next thing you know, you'll look back and see you're not alone.
- Find the teacher with the food. Trust me, you'll need a pick me up sometimes.
- Respect your teachers. You forget they're just doing their job.
- Dear girl: other girls will have something to say. It usually stems from insecurities. Show you're confident with who you are by simply saying nothing at all.
- There's a difference between confidence and pride.
- Think optimistically. Optimism is the key that pushes you towards your goal.
- Girls, have a vent day, but be nice about it. It's good to vent all those feelings out.
- Hard work beats talent when talent doesn't work hard.
- For athletes, remember everyone gets old. Don't forget about your education to fall back on.
- Don't count your chickens before they hatch.

- "No one can make you feel inferior without your consent."- Eleanor Roosevelt
- Respect your teachers. They are here for your benefit.
- THINK! You should think before you act.
- Do to others as you would want them to do to you. Golden Rule.
- It's better to have a hard time with an AP class in high school and get help than to have to take it (and pay for it) in college without the help you get in high school.
- Sit down and relax every now and then. Think about the things you have to do.
- Alcohol and cigarettes might have an age limit, but drugs will never have one.
- Don't take out your anger on other people when it's clearly your fault.
- When you don't care what people think about you, you are usually happier in life.
- Always carry gum. You never know who you might run into.
- Dance a little. It relieves any amount of stress.
- Do not text and drive. The text can wait.
- Don't look back on the past, so you can focus on the present, and have an amazing future.

Fix the Problem!

- Things happen for a reason. Don't question life, just enjoy the ride.
- If you have screwed up, pay the price.
- Don't help people the way you want to help them, help them the way they asked you to help them.
- Find something you enjoy doing and stick to it.
- Talk to new people. You never know who you will meet.
- You can't change the past, so learn from it.
- Always remember that when you're in a bad situation someone else is always in a worse one.
- Do things for yourself because living for others isn't living at all.
- No wise man will ever tell you about the risks he didn't take.
- Don't do something that will embarrass your family and yourself.
- Whatever you do, do it mainly to make yourself proud. Not others.
- Keep calm and keep going! Everything has a solution.
- NEVER EVER let boys get in the way of your schooling.

- People are often unreasonable, irrational, and self- centered. Forgive them anyway. Life is too short for grudges. Hate consumes you.
- Give the best you have and it will never be enough. Give your best anyway. Don't find excuses to give up or not to try. It's seriously a waste of precious time.
- Make time to breathe. Sometimes in the midst of high school it's hard to appreciate the little things, but they are the most special.
- If you are kind, people may accuse you of selfish or having ulterior motives. Be kind anyway. The people who lie and cheat and gossip never make it in the real world. Be yourself and never take your frustration out on others, you'll lose friends.
- Love your life. Milk it for all it's worth.
- Don't procrastinate! Especially with school projects. Your life will be less stressful that way.
- Don't be scared to do something unusual. You'll never know how comfortable you are with something if you never try.
- Always keep an open mind. Even if you completely disagree with something. A new

look on something could change your
perspective forever.
- Take people as they are and don't expect
change and realize no one's here forever.
- Take things a day at a time. Don't look back
and don't peak ahead. The moments you
currently live are the most forgotten.
- Don't worry what other people think of you
because their opinion doesn't matter.
- Don't listen to rumors or gossip because most
of the time it isn't true.
- Don't be quick to jump to conclusion Look for
the facts first.
- Don't put pride in front of a child. If you can't
take care of a child consider alternatives
because you are dealing with a life. Don't
punish the baby because of pride.
- Life is like a painting. You don't understand it
until it has happened.
- Curiosity is the lust of the mind.
- Most important thing in life is learning how to
fail.
- Live in the moment. Cherish the present.
Anticipate the future and frame your
yesterday.

- Smile and there's nothing you can't overcome.
- There's no such thing as coincidence. Everything happens for a reason.
- Make a habit of studying. Laziness will come knocking on your door and bite you in the butt later.
- Get in a habit of reading books. Whatever your fancy is: books, magazines, or whatever. Just read!
- Stay real and true to yourself.
- Always carry an extra pair of shoes in the car.
- Never break a person's heart on purpose.
- Pray every night. It helps and God listens.
- Respect your elders. You never know if you will inherent any money.
- Be ready for anything and everything.
- If you find yourself habitually procrastinating, set an alarm for 3 AM and do all your homework before you would normally wake up.
- If a friendship or relationship disappoints you more than it makes you happy, you should end the relationship.
- Being idealistic, creative, and moderate can fulfill one's own life with success.

- If you can't take the heat, don't go out in the sun.
- Actions always speak louder than words, and laziness is the dark element of human nature.
- Take advantage of your weekends. Enjoy yourself and do something different with different people.
- Register for the SAT/ACT even if the computers at school are really slow.
- Don't focus too much on being well rounded. Find something you truly love and commit.
- When experiencing life's difficulties the only thing you can do is laugh. Not only does it make you feel better, but it takes your mind off the negativity.
- Take care of your body. Once it breaks down, that's it.
- Don't give anyone the power to control your emotions. You will most likely end up bitter and irrational.
- It's good to have a game plan for school. Have a goal.
- Being consistent is the best habit.
- Get your stuff done before it's too late.
- Life is an underrated phenomenon.

- Always give back and expect nothing in return.
- Get ahead now, that way you don't have to worry about tomorrow.
- Do things right the first time.
- Don't date someone until you've gotten to know that person well enough.
- Do something good for someone that doesn't benefit you in any way.
- All things happen for a reason. Don't complain about something that already passed It won't change.
- Do not be afraid to say no!
- Once in awhile, just say no and don't feel guilty. It's okay to be a people pleaser but remember that you should be happy too!
- ALWAYS BE KIND AND RESPECTFUL! Even to your enemies, that annoying kid, or even to that no so attractive looking person who stole your boyfriend/ girlfriend. There is no excuse for you to not be kind or respectful towards others.
- Go to fast food restaurants and tell them it's your birthday to get free food or discounts! The worst they can do it say no.

- High school sucks. It's just something that everyone has to go through. Like a horrible chapter in an amazing story, but if you give up you'll never get to the best part.
- Stop complaining about having no freedom. School and parents are there to train you to survive "real" freedom. Fighting it will only end with you relying on them forever and giving up the freedom you <u>could</u> have had.
- Always kill your food before you eat it even if it's cafeteria food. There's no telling if it's still alive or not so a few stabs with a folk should suffice.
- Deal with stress. Don't let it build up.
- Don't limit yourself. Do everything that you can.
- Do all your homework. It will help you with tests and quizzes.
- Problems. If it happens once, it may never happen again, but if it happens twice it is bound to happen a third time.
- Those who don't learn from history are doomed it repeat it. George Santayana
- The problem with an "eye for an eye" way of thinking is that we all end up blind.

- In your teenage years you will have friends who pressure you to do bad things, but don't fall for it because they are not your friends and they are not looking out for you.
- Don't over think things. It's bad and stressful,. Just stay calm and at the end it will be alright.
- Think more of yourself. If you underestimate yourself you will fail at everything because you think you can't do it.
- Don't be fake. Be yourself.
- Girls... if he doesn't treat you right – he's not worth it. Remember...women in power!!
- Don't let anyone tell you that "you can't." You can do anything you set your mind to.
- Don't be stupid. We call it common sense for a reason.
- Don't discourage yourself when it comes to overcoming a difficult obstacle.
- Prove people wrong when they put you down.
- If you are going to make a mistake, make it a good mistake.
- Nothing's wrong with ordering off the dollar menu. You get more for less.
- Listen to Mr. Liljedahl.
- Stay positive even through life's toughest test.

Fix the Problem!

- Choose your team wisely for group projects. You don't want someone to do nothing and get a good grade for it.
- Don't go to a party the weekend before your project is due. You'll be too hung over to care about your grade.
- When driving, make sure you park your car BEFORE turning it off.
- If someone is on the side of the road and has car trouble, be sure to pull over and help with what you can.
- Don't let yourself, or your friends, do stupid things.
- If you're doing well for yourself, don't let others get in the way.
- If something makes you happy, don't let it slip away.
- Your relationships will not be perfect. There will be problems. Don't be selfish because you will have to make sacrifices to make each other happy.
- Never argue with your mother. You will never win.
- Limit yourself when hanging out with your friends.

- Never make someone a priority if all you are to them is an option.
- Without bad days, you wouldn't appreciate the good ones.
- Patience is the key that unlocks all situations that seem impossible.
- Fears are nothing more than states of mind. The more you fear, the more you limit yourself.
- Don't slack off when everyone else does.
- Don't take your parents or teachers for granted.
- Karma is very real...Always be kind and considerate to others.
- Always have faith in something. Even if you don't believe in religion it will help you throughout life.
- Never think the best of people until they prove to you that they have earned your trust.
- If you had a bad day, don't let it ruin your week! Always think tomorrow will be a better day.
- The worst person you can lie to is yourself.
- Patience might be a relatively long word, but it doesn't always go a long way. Always have a

shoulder available for a friend because you never know when you may need one.

- Don't trust everyone. Not everyone can keep a secret.
- High school life is hard and you're not the only one with problems so be there for your friends.
- Once you're in a relationship, if you split up and it doesn't work the second time, it probably won't work at all.
- Don't fall to hard for someone. There are more people out in the world, and enough time to fall in love.
- Tell people you love them. You never know if you may see them again or not.
- Don't let other people decide who you love. It's your happiness, not theirs.
- Be fearless with the choices you make in life. It could lead to something amazing.
- Your mouth will get you in trouble. Your ears won't.
- Don't get crushes and love confused.
- When others are in trouble or have a problem, try to put yourself in their shoes and see where they're coming from. They may

have a tougher life than you, so be thankful of your life and what you have.

- Never feel lonely in a crowded room. There's always that one person who can make everything feel better.
- Do something nice for someone. Even the smallest act of kindness can affect another in a big way.
- Watch what you say. Words impact more than you think.
- Don't laugh too much during class, it gets annoying!!
- There's a point in your junior year where you're going to get tired of everyone and everything. Everyone goes through that so don't worry. Okay, YES worry, but don't go into depression either!
- Join clubs or organizations like band or choir. You make good friends in there.
- Staying up late will do you no good the next morning.
- Relying on electronic devices isn't really a good thing. What good is it to Google all of the answers to your homework if you're not learning anything?

- It's always good to have some sort of hobby to keep you busy.
- Physics Baby!

ABOUT CURT LILJEDAHL

I am a former physics teacher/diving coach/aquatics director, who with my wife of 32 years, retired financially independent at the ripe old age of 54. Cool huh! I am also the very proud father of two amazing young ladies for whom I wrote this book. Don't get me wrong! My life is far from perfect and I have screwed up more times than I care to think of, but I keep trying to be a better person.

Not perfect...better.

When my oldest daughter was going off to college I got to thinking there was a lot of things I still wanted her to know about so I started writing them down. That led to my Life Lessons that I would teach to my students in the filler times of the school day. My students seemed to enjoy this bit of wisdom very much (maybe because I wasn't talking about Physics???). Finally, one day while driving and teaching my youngest daughter a life lesson she said, "Just write a book Dad!!" You will notice that I sometimes write like I talk, but that is because I am coming from a teacher and father point of view...not a real author!
Please enjoy!

Made in the USA
Columbia, SC
24 August 2019